BROKEN METRONOME

USA TODAY BESTSELLING AUTHOR
PERSEPHONE AUTUMN

BETWEEN WORDS PUBLISHING LLC

BROKEN METRONOME

USA TODAY BESTSELLING AUTHOR
PERSEPHONE AUTUMN

BETWEEN WORDS PUBLISHING LLC

Broken Metronome

Copyright © 2021 by Persephone Autumn

www.persephoneautumn.com

All rights reserved.

No part of this book may be reproduced in any form or by any electronic or mechanical means, including photocopying, information storage and retrieval systems, without written permission from the author except for the use of brief quotations in a book review. No part of this book may be used to create, feed, or refine artificial intelligence models, for any purpose, without written consent from the author.

This book is a work of fiction. Names, characters, establishments, organizations, and incidents are either products of the author's imagination or are used fictitiously to give a sense of authenticity. Any resemblance to actual events, places, or persons, living or dead, is entirely coincidental.

If you're reading this book and did not purchase it, or it was not purchased for your use only, or it was purchased on a site I do not advertise I sell on, then it was pirated illegally. Please purchase a copy of your own on a platform where the author advertises she distributes and respect the hard work of this author.

ISBN: 978-1-951477-16-5 (Ebook)

ISBN: 978-1-951477-17-2 (Paperback)

Editor: Ellie McLove | My Brother's Editor

Cover Design: Persephone Autumn | Between Words Publishing LLC

BOOKS BY PERSEPHONE AUTUMN

LAKE LAVENDER SERIES

Depths Awakened

One Night Forsaken

Every Thought Taken

DEVOTION SERIES

Distorted Devotion

Undying Devotion

Beloved Devotion

Darkest Devotion

Sweetest Devotion

BAY AREA DUET SERIES

<u>Click Duet</u>

Through the Lens

Time Exposure

<u>Inked Duet</u>

Fine Line

Love Buzz

Insomniac Duet

Restless Night

A Love So Bright

Artist Duet

Blank Canvas

Abstract Passion

Novellas

Reese

Penny

STONE BAY SERIES

Broken Sky—Prequel

Shattered Sun

Fractured Night

Fallen Stars

Stolen Dreams

Raptured Souls

Tethered Hearts

Fiery Storm

STANDALONE ROMANCE NOVELS

Sweet Tooth

Transcendental

In Knots For You

POETRY COLLECTIONS

Ink Veins

Broken Metronome

Slipping From Existence

Poisonous Heart

Beneath Wildflowers

Chemicals Between Us

PUBLISHED UNDER P. AUTUMN

STANDALONE NON-ROMANCE NOVELS

By Dawn

To the past
To the memories of a ghost

CONTENTS

From Afar	1
Endless	3
First Touch	5
Everywhere	7
Fantasy	9
Push	11
Pull	13
Hello, Again	15
Periphery	17
Almost Forgotten	19
False Seduction	21
Percussion	23
Late Night Interlude	25
First Step	27
Last Step	29
Empty Years	31
Broken Silence	33
Cyclone	35
Broken Metronome	37
Thank You	39
More by Persephone	41
Connect with Persephone	45
Acknowledgments	47
About the Author	49

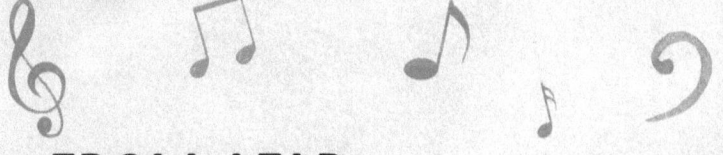

FROM AFAR

Always the shy girl
I watched you from afar
The confidence in your step
How your eyes glinted mine
Always tempting
Teasing
Silently calling out to me
But you never said a word
Not until it was too late
Not until it was impossible
Although I considered
the possibility
of taking a risk
of stepping out of line
but I'm not that girl
So, I sit here
Watch you from afar
Daydreaming
About what if

ENDLESS

We saw each other
time and again
Ran in the same circles
Inevitable friends
But the way you
looked at me
smiled at me
lingered too long
Being friends
had never been in
the cards
the stars
And to this day
when I close my eyes
your smile brightens
the endless dark

FIRST TOUCH

I remember that night
the crowd
the music
You sat closer to me
with your addictive smile
Hand under the table
a slight lean forward
and right
Reaching for my knee
The brush of your knuckles
on the length of my thigh
Skin to skin
you made me high
Heartbeat wild
Sweat slicked skin
Breath erratic
I wanted to let you in
But once again
time wasn't right
Always the enemy
pushing us aside

EVERYWHERE

We swim in circles
to and fro
No matter
which way I turn
I see you
everywhere
Not an illusion
or trick of the mind
But a sad
strange reality
Where you exist
to never be mine
Always in my sight
Just out of reach
The smile on your lips
Steals the breath from me
No way to escape
the vision of you
I see you everywhere
I have lost control

FANTASY

Thought of that night
Over
and over
Lifeless in bed
I conjured up visions
of what-ifs
and why nots
Wondering how I got here
Asking how to
go forward
Peeled away ceilings
fade away
as I drift into
a fantasy life
The place where
nothing hurts
or breaks my heart
or makes me numb
A place where
peace begets laughter
and my heart smiles

What a nice
fantasy
One I never wish
to leave

PUSH

Temptation hovered
like a live wire
Jumping
Sparking
Ready to burn
Calling out to me
Teasing
Taunting
An urge to
go against
every moral line
I've ever drawn
Pushing me
to corrupt
who I am
Who I've always been
Just for
a taste
of something
I can never have

PULL

Always in the background
You and me
How it has always been
Imaginary pull
Hidden
Dormant
Waiting
But you're always there
A shadow in the night
Tugging
Pulling
Far
But a little close too

HELLO, AGAIN

Innocent
at first
A simple word
A kind gesture
Small trickle
Like the start of
a summer rainstorm
Minor hints
Flashes
Like heat lightning
Illuminating
the possibilities
of what
you think may be
Hello, Again
Remember me

PERIPHERY

Always there
Lingering
Just in
the periphery
A breath away
With a wide smile
on soft lips
A gentle heart
on your sleeve
A rasp
in your voice
that makes me
weak
in the knees
Always
on the side
Just out of reach
Lingering
Skirting the periphery

ALMOST FORGOTTEN

Years passed by
and I almost forgot
your addictive smile
soulful eyes
the timbre of your voice
Until you
snuck in
and reminded me
Giving me
another dose
of something
I can never have
A tease
A glimpse
It took years
to almost forget
And now
who knows when
I will again

FALSE SEDUCTION

In early spring
you sought me out
With endearing words
and the smile
you knew I'd love
Mentions of
longing
pining
Keywords
every girl
wishes to hear
Playing with
my fragile heart
with flirtation and
promises
How easily I fell
for your
perversion and
false seduction

PERCUSSION

I'd never really dated
Never took things slow
But with you
I wanted to
savor the taste
Roll it
on my tongue
Let it
consume me
unlike anything else
You were different
Or so I believed
The way you kick-started
my pulse
my breath
and awakened
desire in my veins
My circadian rhythm
learning a new
percussion
I wanted to
take things slow

Prove I had
more to give
That I wasn't just
another itch to scratch
another easy girl
I thought you were different
With the flutter
you provoked
inside me
But my naivety
blinded me
and set me up
again
for another letdown

LATE NIGHT INTERLUDE

For several years
I hid myself
from life
and love
and carnal desire
Somehow
you brought them all
to the surface
With your late-night
Interludes
Sweet and naughty
words
and images
Making me crave you
more than ever before
I miss those
balmy spring nights
When I briefly felt
wanted
desirable
precious

FIRST STEP

You invite me out
Wanted to explore
the possibility
of you and me
And I went
eagerly
with a smile on my lips
and in my eyes
Sat across from you
Talked
Shared a meal
Thought
this is what it's like
dating
Such a foreign
concept
feeling
To be more than
just a girl
in someone's bed
Thought of more than
just another lay

It was the
first step
And in that moment
I thought there would be
many more

LAST STEP

We met up
for a night of fun
Music
Laughter
A chance to
know more
about each other
I remember the
hope
that flowed
through my veins
The flutter
beneath my diaphragm
The buzz
inside my ribcage
And the thought of
how perfect
it all felt
When we said
goodnight
I wanted to kiss you
under the moon

in that parking lot
But neither of us
made the move
to lean closer
press our lips together
explore uncharted waters
And soon
I would learn
that was our
last step
last opportunity
last chance

EMPTY YEARS

Time
a manmade concept
Ticks
ticks
ticks
The rhythm of
a metronome
slow
steady
constant
And through the
empty years
it ticks louder
A reminder of
what was
what is
what will never be
An inescapable
tick
tick
tick
I shove it down

Blanket it with
reality
And hope one day
the empty years
will fade away

BROKEN SILENCE

Out of nowhere
Your name appeared
again
A specter
in the night
Haunting
Torturing
Disturbing
my soul
Your appearance
innocent
No hidden meaning
A friendly
hello
how are you
are you happy
And I said
yes
I am
I was
I will find a way
to be

happy
Because happiness is
a state of mind
a central focus
within my control
But I wish
you wouldn't have
broken the silence
I wish you
would have remained
a ghost of the past
a forgotten thought
Tucked away
in the cobwebs
of my mind
Never to be
unleashed
remembered
felt again
Go back to
silence
Let me rest
in peace

CYCLONE

It drives me
mad
The cyclone
in my head
my heart
Swirling
Raging
Stirring up
earth
thought
questions without answers
Questions I
shouldn't ask
What-ifs
Why nots
Because the answers
don't matter
never have
never will
Yet I choose
to torture
my mind

my heart
my soul
A glutton
for pain
for pleasure
for punishment
Over
and over
and over
Like the constant swirl
of the cyclone
Until I'm too tired
physically
emotionally
Until I give in
give up
let go

BROKEN METRONOME

The end is here
Silence abounds
No more
tick
tick
tick
Just a
broken metronome
Absence is
shitty
crushing
normal
for the best
But the glimmer never
fades
disappears
leaves for good
In its place
I look for new ways
to smile
to laugh
to learn

to accept
All things happen with purpose
Not all things
are meant to last
Not all music
is meant to be played
Not all hearts
are meant to be loved
And just like the
tick
tick
tick
of the metronome
Not all beats
carry on
make new songs
last forever
Some beats
will forever be
broken

THANK YOU

Thank you so much for reading Broken Metronome, my second poetry collection. If you would take a moment to leave a review on the retailer site where you made your purchase, Goodreads and/or BookBub, it would mean the world to me.

Reviews help other readers find and enjoy the book as well.

Much love,
    Persephone

MORE BY PERSEPHONE

Ink Veins
Persephone Autumn's debut poetry collection, Ink Veins, explores topics of depression, love, and self-discovery with a raw, unfiltered voice.

Slipping From Existence
Would it be so bad to slip from existence? Would it be so bad to give in to the darkness?
Slipping From Existence is a dark poetry collection centered around depression and coping while maintaining a brave face.

Poisonous Heart
Drip fed, little by little, I was young when I got my first taste of poison.
Small doses in heart-shaped packages labeled as love.
I don't remember the very first taste. But that's how poison works.

Beneath Wildflowers

You were the sweetest, most precious surprise.
A soul with a tender heart.
I will love and miss you forever.
As you rest beneath the wildflowers.

Chemicals Between Us

During the most significant years of my life,
you were mine
and nothing else mattered.

The Click Duet

High school sweethearts torn apart. When fate gives them a second chance, one doesn't trust they won't be hurt again. Through the Lens (Click Duet #1) and Time Exposure (Click Duet #2) is an angsty, second chance, friends to lovers romance with all the feels.

Every Thought Taken

As young children, an unshakable friendship brought them together. As teens, they discovered an undeniable love. Then life pulled them in different directions–into darkness and light–and slowly ripped them apart. Years later, he returns home in the hopes of a second chance with his first love and to conquer the demons of his past.

Transcendental

A musician in search of his muse and a woman grieving

the loss of her husband. Two weeks at an exclusive retreat and their connection rivals all others. Until she leaves early without notice. But he refuses to give up until he finds her again.

Broken Sky

Their eyes meet across the bar, but she looks away first. Does her best to give him zero attention. But when he crowds her on the dancefloor, she can't deny the instant chemistry. After one night together, he marks her as his. Unfortunately, another woman thinks he belongs to her.

Shattered Sun

When your heart is split in two, how do choose who to love more? While Ben, her childhood best friend, and Travis, the hottest cop in Stone Bay, fight for Kirsten's affection, someone else has their eye on her. When she questions everyone and everything, Ben and Travis vow to protect her. In the process, she falls for both men. Before it's too late, she needs to decide which man she loves more.

CONNECT WITH PERSEPHONE

Connect with Persephone
www.persephoneautumn.com

Subscribe to Persephone's Newsletter
www.persephoneautumn.com/newsletter

Join Persephone's Reader Group
Persephone's Playground

Follow Persephone Online

- instagram.com/persephoneautumn
- facebook.com/persephoneautumnwrites
- tiktok.com/@persephoneautumn
- bookbub.com/authors/persephone-autumn
- goodreads.com/persephoneautumn
- amazon.com/author/persephoneautumn
- pinterest.com/persephoneautumn
- threads.com/@persephoneautumn

ACKNOWLEDGMENTS

To my family… Thank you for continually supporting my dream to write and publish. To my daughter, for being the most amazing young woman I've ever known and supporting me as much as I do you. I wouldn't be who I am without you. To my dad, for being the best dad a girl or woman could ask for. No matter what, you always lift me up. I love you all more than words!

To my editor, Ellie… Whenever I email you with poetry, I wonder if it bores you to read such small "manuscripts" or if you like the simplicity. No matter what, you always rock out my words!

To my reader group… Thank you for reading and loving my words. For continuing to pick up my books. Thank you for chatting with me and being my friend. Bookish people are the best people, and I love you!

To my author friends… Every day, I am grateful to know you and thankful to have you in my life. Writing is the easy part (mostly), it's all the other stuff that makes us crazy. You all make the crazy much more tolerable… and fun!

To all the readers… Thank you for buying my book. Thank you for reading my words. I remain humbled (and not so secretly squeal like a school girl) every time someone purchases my books. Thank you is not a big enough sentiment to express my gratitude. Sending you all tons of hugs and all the love!

ABOUT THE AUTHOR

USA Today Bestselling Author Persephone Autumn is a proud mom with a cuckoo grandpup. An ethnic food enthusiast who has fun discovering ways to vegan-ize her favorite non-vegan foods. Most days, you'll find her with a tea latte or fruity concoction in her hand. If given the opportunity, she would intentionally get lost in nature.

For years, Persephone did some form of writing; mostly journaling or poetry. After pairing her poetry with images and posting them online, she began the journey of writing her first novel.

She mainly writes romance and poetry, but on occasion dips her toes in other works. Look for her non-romance novel publications under P. Autumn.

www.ingramcontent.com/pod-product-compliance
Lightning Source LLC
Chambersburg PA
CBHW030139100526
44592CB00011B/954